healing:
GOD'S FORGOTTEN GIFT

DR. DAVID STEWART
DON CLAIR
SANDY SUTTER

CONTENTS

Introduction 1

Session 1—Healing: God's Gift from the Beginning 3

Session 2—Oils and Healing 9

Session 3—Oils for Spiritual Purposes 15

Session 4—Cedarwood and Solomon 23

Session 5—Oils, Temple Maintenance, and Repair 29

Session 6—Healing and Repentance 35

Session 7—Faith, Love, Prayer, Oils 43

Session 8—The Great Commission and Beyond 51

Small Group Leader Guide 59

Leader's Notes Session 1 71

Leader's Notes Session 2 75

Leader's Notes Session 3 81

Leader's Notes Session 4 87

Leader's Notes Session 5 91

Leader's Notes Session 6 97

Leader's Notes Session 7 101

Leader's Notes Session 8 105

Final Note for Leaders 107

Resources 108

Class Resources: 111

    Health Assessment 111

    Group Agreement 113

    Calendar 114

    Prayer & Praise Report 115

    Roster 116

About the Authors 117

Where to Obtain Biblical Grade Oils for Healing 120

Answers for Fill-In Blanks 121

What would it mean to you to know that God had a plan from the beginning of time to heal our physical, emotional and spiritual needs? This study will allow you to fully grasp, share, and see clearly the resources God made readily available before the existence of man. Sadly, we have chosen not to see or use these resources. The goal of *Healing: God's Forgotten Gift* is for you to discover and experience the gifts God has given to us to restore and heal the physical and emotional body. Dr. David Stewart, author of *Healing Oils of the Bible*, will place you firmly on a journey that will provide you the opportunity to fully understand, "God's perfect will is not to heal you; His perfect will is that you don't get sick to begin with."

At the time of this writing our world is in a health crisis. Simply walk into any store, look at the person next to you and ask yourself if they are healthy. Or the next time you look at yourself in the mirror, ask, "Am I healthy?" In nearly every newscast there is another report stating how bad our health is in the world. In March 2010, the Center for Disease Control reports a grim picture of our state of health and what we are all facing in the future. In the United States economy, one job out of every seven is somehow related to the healthcare industry. This data identifies either a commitment to keeping people healthy or an investment in people staying in poor health.

We are excited your group is joining us for this journey. God has already given us so many gifts to keep us healthy. His desire is for each of us to experience healing and health at a spiritual, physical and emotional level. The place to start is to fully expect a miracle of healing to take place in your life. Our belief is in the coming weeks miracles will occur.

With a prayer of expectation, let's begin!

Session 1

HEALING: GOD'S GIFT FROM THE BEGINNING

Have you ever considered what would be the perfect environment for mankind? God did that and much more when He
placed Adam and Eve into the Garden of Eden. It was the perfect place for them to live, work, play, and fully experience life.
It was also a spiritual environment where God could stay in close
communication and contact with His children. Think about it:
the Garden of Eden was a place filled with first encounters.

Many view God's Garden (Genesis 3:10) as the place where everything began to fall apart. However, we will soon discover how
everything began for the purpose of serving mankind. God set
Adam and Eve into the Garden and immediately gave them a job
to do! You are now being given the opportunity to consider the
long-term effects of being in the Garden of Eden. God gives us
all an opportunity and a responsibility to experience one of His
very first gifts—present in Eden and still with us today.

Not only does God give physical gifts for our health and wellbe-
ing, He also gives spiritual gifts for us as tools to serve others.
In his first letter to the church of Corinth, the Apostle Paul lists
gifts that are part of the overall body of Christ's Church. He
clarifies that these gifts are given to us by God and we should
desire whatever gift God chooses to give. In Chapter 12, verse 31
Paul writes, "covet earnestly the best gifts." These words provide
direction for us to follow, meaning the best gifts are the ones
that serve others and thereby build up the body of Christ.

As Dr. Stewart shares with us today, God created mankind and provided everything needed to live a rich, full and healthy life. He provided means by which to serve one another, love one another and offer healing to one another by His grace. As God's children we are to pray for all the gifts God desires to give us and use them to His glory, which includes the gift of healing!

SCRIPTURE READINGS

Then God said, "Let the earth put forth vegetation: plants yielding seed, and fruit trees of every kind on earth that bear fruit with the seed in it." And it was so. . . And God saw that it was good. And there was evening and there was morning, the third day. Genesis 1:11-13

So God created man in His own image, in the image of God created He him; male and female created He them. And God blessed them . . . And the Lord God took the man and put him into the Garden of Eden to dress it and to keep it. Genesis 1:27-28; 2:15

On the banks, on both sides of the river, there will grow all kinds of trees for food. . . their fruit will be for food, and their leaves for medicine. Ezekiel 47:12

. . . and the leaves of the tree are for the healing of the nations. Revelation 22:2

Now you are the body of Christ, and members in particular. And God has set some in the church, first apostles, secondarily prophets, thirdly teachers, after that miracles, then gifts of healings…covet earnestly the best gifts. I Corinthians 12:27-28, 31

Proclaim the good news, 'The kingdom of heaven has come near.' Cure the sick, raise the dead, cleanse the lepers, cast out demons. Matthew 10:7-8

WATCH SESSION 1 OF DVD

Why must we desire and pray for God's best Gifts? Why doesn't God just anoint us with the gifts He wants us to express as His will and plan for us? Why must we ask?

- God respects our _____ as His children to whom He has given free _____ and He will not trespass on our _____.
- It is through the process of our _____ and our _____ by which we clear the way and open ourselves to accept whatever God wishes to place within us.
- Possession of this gift does not make us _____. Only _____ heals.

PERSONAL NOTES AND "AHA!" MOMENTS

_____

_____

_____

_____

_____

_____

Discussion Questions

1. Why do you think millions of people visit national parks and other preserves of nature every year? What has been your greatest experience in nature?

2. What instructions did God give to Adam for the care of the Garden of Eden? (Genesis 2:15) What kind of work do you think he and Eve did?

3. What would Adam and Eve need to know in order to care for God's garden? How would this knowledge serve them?

4. Why do you think God placed Adam and Eve in a garden, knowing that He could have placed them in a house, a castle, or any place He chose?

5. What about the Garden of our Human Body with which God has endowed each of us? Do you think the kind of work God assigned to Adam and Eve extended to "dressing and keeping" the Eden of their bodily habitats?

6. Adam and Eve's original sin set mankind on a very difficult path (Genesis 3:1-7). Do you think God knew Adam and Eve were going to sin? Why or why not?

7. Have you known anyone to take an aspirin for pain? Did the aspirin work? How do we know about this method for relieving pain?

8. What do you believe the main illnesses were in Biblical times? Did they have medicines in Biblical times? What do you think they were?

9. Is it possible for things to affect you mentally, emotionally, physically, and health-wise without you knowing that your body's functions are being affected? Share any experiences you may have had with this.

10. In your opinion, is there a difference between learning how to become a teacher and learning to become a healer? Do you believe it's possible to learn and seek to be a healer or is it a gift that is only bestowed by God at His whim with or without your desire or your asking for it?

$\mathcal{S}ession\ 2$

OILS AND HEALING

Healing . . . is it really possible in all cases? This question has haunted mankind since Adam and Eve were expelled from the Garden of Eden. We all know people with disease who have prayed and been prayed for by their church congregations who have not been healed. Why is this? Are there pre-requisites to being healed? Did Jesus heal everyone or was He selective? Should we go out seeking people to heal or should we wait for them to come to us? How do we know the difference between those who would be receptive to spiritual healing and those for whom even many prayers and anointings would not help? What should we do when people reject our offers of healing prayer and anointing according to Biblical principles?

In addition to His twelve disciples, Jesus commissioned many others to go forth and heal, but did they do it by prayer alone or did they apply physical medicines as well? Did Jesus' call for His followers to engage in a healing mission end 2000 years ago or does it extend to us today?

The verses in Mark and James are pivotal points in the spreading of Christ's message. They associate repentance and confession of sins with healing, which we will discuss in more detail later in Session Six of these studies. Mark and James also specify that in combination with prayer, anointing with oils was also to be part of the process for spiritual healing. The Bible does not mention any instance of Jesus, Himself, anointing with oils for healing, but His disciples did and so did the members of the early church for centuries afterwards. Why would application of essential oils be advised for healing by Christ's followers and not for Christ, Himself? Why not just prayer?

Dr. Stewart's questions will require some real self-reflection like, "where do you go first when you become ill? Where, what or in whom do you put your trust when illness strikes? "

SCRIPTURE READINGS

He called the twelve and began to send them out two by two, and gave them authority over the unclean spirits . . . He said to them, "Whenever you enter a house, stay there until you leave the place. If any place will not welcome you and they refuse to hear you, as you leave, shake off the dust that is on your feet as a testimony against them." So they went out and proclaimed that all should repent. They cast out many demons, and anointed with oil many who were sick and healed them. Mark 6:7, 10-13.

After this the Lord appointed seventy others and sent them on ahead of him in pairs to every town and place where he himself intended to go. He said to them, "The harvest is plentiful, but the laborers are few; . . . whenever you enter a town and its people welcome you, eat what is set before you; cure the sick who are there, and say to them, 'The kingdom of God has come near to you' but whenever you enter a town and they do not welcome you, go out into its streets and say, 'Even the dust of your town that clings to our feet, we wipe off in protest against you." Luke 10:1-2, 8-11

Is there any sick among you? Let him call for the elders of the church; and let them pray over him, anointing him with oil in the name of the Lord. . . confess your faults one to another, and pray one for another, that you may be healed. The effectual fervent prayer of a righteous man avails much. James 5:14, 16.

WATCH SESSION 2 ON DVD

Why should we incorporate oils into our healing mission? Why not just prayer? If God is the source of healing, then why do we need to anoint with oils?

- Jesus' disciples were instructed by Jesus, Himself, to _____ in healing.
- If it is Jesus' instructions to apply oils as part of the healing process, then it follows that we should make the effort to _____ the oils and _____ how to _____ effectively.
- It is our place to make ourselves _____ as willing healers.
- It is the place of the sick person to _____ and our duty to _____ when rejected or when people are not interested.
- We can pray for God to _____ them and open their _____.

PERSONAL NOTES AND "AHA!" MOMENTS

_____
_____
_____
_____
_____
_____

Discussion Questions

I. Have you ever prayed for someone to be well and they did not get well? Why do you think your prayer was not answered with healing as you requested?

2. Have you ever prayed for someone to be well by yourself or with a group and they were cured in response to your prayer? What was the difference between your successful prayer and your unsuccessful one?

3. Have you ever been very sick and people have prayed over you and yet you remained ill? Why do you think the prayers of the others were not answered as both you and they wished?

4. When you become ill where and how do you seek healing first? Do you call the doctor or 911? Do you call the elders of the church to pray, lay on hands, and anoint with oil for your healing? Why or why not?

5. Building on what you learned from Dr. Stewart do you believe there is room in modern medicine for anointing and other applications of essential oils? Why or why not?

6. How might consistent negative emotions bring about illness in the body? Have you ever seen this happen in your life or in someone else's?

7. What happens to your body when you harbor persistent feelings of jealously, unforgiveness, resentment, anger, pity, poor self-worth, or frustration?

8. In the first century it was a common Hebrew custom to connect sin to illness. Is that pattern of thought still with us today? Why or why not?

9. After reading Mark 6:13, what affect do you believe prayer and being anointed with oils might have on you?

10. If you offer to lay on hands, anoint with oil, and pray for someone's illness according to the manner described in Mark and James and your offer is refused, what should you do next?

Session 3

OILS FOR SPIRITUAL PURPOSES

In the book of Exodus God speaks directly to Moses so His message will be heard exactly as He intends. What is God's message? Very specific instructions for making "the Holy Anointing Oil" that was to be used for consecrating (dedicating, setting apart as holy) the priests and temple objects. God goes on to give Moses a specific formula for a Holy Incense that is to be used "in front of the Testimony in the Tent of Meeting" (Exodus 30:36).

Both of these formulas were to be the work of a "perfumer" or "apothecary." These titles refer to priests specially trained to harvest herbs, distill oils, assemble the ingredients, and compound the incense and anointing oil for temple use. Perfumery is still a profession today. Perfumers are very special in that many of them have trained their noses to distinguish as many as 2,000 aromatic compounds.

Aromas can have a direct effect upon ones spiritual, emotional and physical health. God knew this since He created us with the amazing ability to recall exact moments of powerful events associated with the memory of a smell. It is also noteworthy for us to consider that God's aromatic formula was pleasing to Him. (Exodus 30:31)

The priests and Israelites would have experienced the effects of both the anointing oil and incense on their physical bodies as well as the environment when they entered the temple. Consider for a moment that during this time mankind lived in a very difficult and harsh environment. The non-existent sanitation caused many different illnesses and diseases. The Israelites' experience with disease would have caused fear, isolation and despair and lead them to experience the feeling, "Is God here with us?"

The temple was a place where sacrifices were offered daily. For example, in Jesus' day, during the week of Passover hundreds of thousands of animals were sacrificed in Jerusalem. The sacrifice of any life leaves behind matter that promotes the growth of pathogens that can cause disease. God's aromatic anointing oil and incense not only hold secrets that served ancient man but we will learn how they can serve us today. One of God's first gifts may be what again preserves mankind's existence.

SCRIPTURE REFERENCES

The Lord spoke to Moses: Take the finest spices: of liquid myrrh five hundred shekels, and of sweet-smelling cinnamon half as much, that is, too hundred fifty, and two hundred fifty of aromatic cane (calamus), and five hundred of cassia—measured by the sanctuary shekel—and a hin of olive oil; and you shall make of these a sacred anointing oil blended as by the perfumer; it shall be a holy anointing oil. With it you shall anoint the tent of meeting and the ark of the covenant, and the table and all its utensils, and the lampstand and its utensils, and the altar of incense, and the altar of burnt offering with all its utensils, and the basin with its stand; you shall consecrate them, so that they may be most holy; whatever touches them will become holy. You shall anoint Aaron and his sons, and consecrate them, in order that they may serve me as priests. You shall say to the Israelites, "This shall be my holy anointing oil throughout your generations." Exodus 30:22-31

The Lord said to Moses: Take sweet spices, stacte (myrrh), and onycha, and galbanum, sweet spices with pure frankincense (an equal part of each), and make an incense blended as by the perfumer, seasoned with salt, pure and holy; and you shall beat some of it into powder, and put part of it before the covenant in the tent of meeting (Tabernacle) where I shall meet with you; it shall be for you most holy. Exodus 30:34-36

Then Samuel took the horn of oil, and anointed him in the presence of his brothers: and the spirit of the Lord came mightily upon David from that day forward. I Samuel 16:13

There the priest Zadok took the horn of oil from the tent and anointed Solomon. . . and all the people said, "Long live King Solomon!" I Kings 1:39

Thou anointest my head with oil. Psalm 23:5

WATCH SESSION 3 ON DVD

If God so thoughtfully prescribed aromatic oils for the Old Testament people, not only as a means to uplift their spirits and enable them to more easily pray and communicate with Him, but also as a means to protect themselves from the pathogens that could arise from daily animal sacrifice, consider this: Could it also be possible that God, in His loving thoughtfulness, also had in mind that we apply His oils today for health, protection, and healing in our daily lives beyond the sanctuary?

- You will find that if you _____ in using essential oils, God will answer.
- If you are receptive and listening, He will _____ whatever it is that you need to know.
- God knows more about the _____ than any person or book. He _____ them!

PERSONAL NOTES AND "AHA!" MOMENTS

_____

_____

_____

_____

_____

_____

Discussion Questions

1. Does the aroma of cinnamon, lemonade, cedar trees, or apple pie bring back memories to you? Share a time when you smelled something that brought back a flood of memories. Can you see it in your mind? Was the experience emotionally pleasant or difficult?

2. What kinds of disease could be spread because of blood sacrifices?

3. Was the plague among the Israelites described in Numbers 16:46-50 due to the environment created by regular animal sacrifice? If not, then what was the cause?

4. What was God's prescription to protect the Old Testament priests from the potential pathogens that could proliferate on a site of daily animal sacrifice?

5. Do you think Moses or the Israelites understood the anti-microbial protections provided by the oils and the incense?

6. What kind of medical evidence was required to experience healing during Moses' time?

7. Dr. Stewart allowed us all insight on how God provided
    solutions to life's greatest challenge with the smallest of
    elements like the tiny, invisible molecules of essential oils.
    Share a time when something powerful arrived in your life
    that was so small you almost overlooked the blessing.

8. With what you learned from Dr. Stewart today how do you
    now view the power of aromatic oils and their possible prac-
    tical uses for us today?

9. How is the use of God's provision of anointing oil and
    incense part of His plan for healing the sick, preventing
    disease and keeping mankind spiritually connected?

10. Why do you think the medical system today has not openly
    or widely adopted the use of essential oils for treatments,
    cures, and healing?

Session 4

CEDARWOOD AND SOLOMON

Scripture tells us that King Solomon was one of the wisest people to have ever lived (1 Kings 3:5, 7-12; 4:29-34). Reading these Scripture passages one tends to always focus on how Solomon provided the best wisdom, the wisest leadership choices and sought out knowledge. Solomon, from the first day of his reign, asked God for wisdom. One of Solomon's wisest choices in temple building materials may seem unimportant on the surface; however, this decision changed the course of Israel's relationship with God. (1 Kings 5)

Have you ever asked, "Why would Solomon choose cedarwood to build God's temple?" Cedarwood would have been the most expensive building material of Solomon's time and the most difficult to obtain. The King of Israel would have had multiple choices in construction material that would have resulted in a beautiful long lasting structure. Closer study will show Solomon chose wisely.

The new king of Israel was aware of the long history and value of cedarwood as his father, King David, used it for the building of his own palace. Solomon would have known the Egyptians use of the wood for preserving documents and how insects had a natural dislike for aroma. He intuitively knew that cedarwood did more than work well as a construction material; it also had effects on mental thought. Solomon knew that the cedarwood would in fact be valued as much as a king's ransom in creating a structure worthy to come within and worship God.

This long-lasting aromatic substance did more than simply preserve cloth, scrolls and worldly treasures; its fragrance cleared the mental passages of those who came to worship God in this temple.

Furthermore, cedarwood oil mixed with hyssop served as a medicinal oil. It was the formula which God gave to Moses for leprosy and a variety of rashes, swellings, eruptions, and diseases of the skin which, in modern terms, could include psoriasis, skin cancers, and even some tumors. (Leviticus 14:54)

Every encounter with cedarwood would serve as a reminder of the gifts provided to the Israelites by God.

SCRIPTURE REFERENCES

The trees of the Lord are watered abundantly, the cedars of Lebanon that he planted. Psalm 104:16

The Lord spoke to Moses, saying: This shall be the ritual for the leprous person at the time of his cleansing . . . the priest shall command that two living clean birds and cedarwood and crimson yarn and hyssop be brought for the one who is to be cleansed . . . the priest shall take some of the log (2/3 of a pint) of oil and pour it into the palm of his own left hand, and dip his right finger in the oil that is in his left hand and sprinkle some oil with his finger seven times before the Lord. Some of the oil that remains in his hand the priest shall put on the right ear of the one to be cleansed, and on the thumb of the right hand, and on the big toe of the right foot . . . the rest of the oil that is in the priest's hand he shall put on the head of the one to be cleansed. Then the priest shall make atonement on his behalf before the Lord . . . this is the ritual for any leprous disease: for an itch, for leprous diseases in clothing and houses, and for a swelling or an eruption or a spot. Leviticus 14:1-2, 4, 15-18, 54.

And he built the walls of the house within with boards of cedar, both the floor of the house and the walls of the ceiling. I Kings 6:15

WATCH SESSION 4 ON DVD

While it is always appropriate to pray directly to God for clarity in our thinking and accuracy in our understanding, does it make sense to apply a mentally enhancing aroma, created by God, to assist us in our praying, in our studies and in our thinking? If the scent of cedarwood was good for King Solomon, does it make sense that we could also benefit from the using cedarwood oil?

- It does not diminish our _____ to apply the gifts of His creation, such as His essential oils, for:

- _____

- Enhancement of our _____, or

- For the enabling of our_____ to be more focused and effective.

PERSONAL NOTES AND "AHA!" MOMENTS

_____

_____

_____

_____

_____

_____

Discussion Questions

1. Have you ever been inside a closet lined with cedar? Why use cedar? Where would builders have learned about this?

2. What are some common household items that may contain cedarwood oil?

3. Dr. Stewart discussed how cedarwood can help with mental blockages. Share a time you or someone you know experienced a mental or spiritual blockage.

4. God gave a healing blend of oils to Moses for treatment of "leprous diseases." It was composed of the oils of Cedarwood and Hyssop. Can you think of any diseases today that might be relieved with this oil? Would you use it?

5. In your opinion why would David and Solomon plant cedar trees throughout the city of Jerusalem?

6. Cedarwood has a long history of being used for construction material. What were some of the ancient uses for cedarwood by the Egyptians?

7. What was the cost for Israel to use cedarwood for the construction of the Temple? Discuss cost vs. the benefit of Solomon's decision.

8. How did people know in ancient times that cedarwood was something that would protect the body from disease-carrying insects and bugs?

9. What must it have been like to live every day in an environment that supported and amplified your wisdom?

10. How might you create an environment today that would support wise choices?

$\mathcal{S}ession\ 5$

OILS, TEMPLE MAINTENANCE AND REPAIR

The scripture readings from this week compare our bodies to a Temple: a physical structure made of brick, mortar, wood and stone; a place where God dwells, lives inside, and meets His people. Through this comparison we learn what God truly wants us to know about ourselves and how He provides tools for maintaining our own temples.

Outward appearances of buildings or houses often give an indication of whether the structure is or is not well maintained. Whenever you see one that is not, do you ever wonder why the property owner did not provide adequate care for the building? Did it become too difficult to keep up? Does it hold bad memories? Did it become outdated? Or did the cost of maintenance simply become too much of a sacrifice? The parallel here between our bodies and the structural temple is similar. God asks each of us to treat our bodies as a temple, a holy place where He dwells. Often we view this simply as our physical bodies. However, let's take it one step further.

If someone asked you to touch the sides of your head on each side of your face, what would you call that area of the body? We refer to this as our "temples." Our mind is also our personal temple. So not only are we called upon to keep our bodily temples clean and maintained, we are also called upon to keep our mental temples clean and clear to express God's Holy Spirit. God wants to be a part of each of us. One of our greatest challenges in life is keeping our temple well maintained so that it is a healthy place fit for spiritual sacrifices and for God to dwell and commune with us.

Today we will be evaluating the condition of our own temples as well as learning about some of the maintenance tools God provides for us. During this time we will also learn how much God desires for us all to keep our temples, both mental and physical, a healthy, pure, and holy place.

SCRIPTURE REFERENCES

As a man thinks in his heart, so is he. Proverbs 23:7

Love . . . thinks no evil. I Corinthians 13:5

Behold, the kingdom of God is within you. Luke 17:21

You are the temple of the living God. II Corinthians 6:16

Beloved, I wish above all things that you may prosper and be in health, even as your soul prospers. III John 2.

Do you not know that you are God's temple and that God's Spirit dwells in you? If anyone destroys God's temple, God will destroy that person. For God's temple is holy, and you are that temple. I Corinthians 3:16-17.

Do you not know that your body is a temple of the Holy Spirit within you, which you have from God, and that you are not your own? I Corinthians 6:19

Like living stones, let yourselves be built into a spiritual house, to be a holy priesthood, to offer spiritual sacrifices acceptable to God through Jesus Christ. I Peter 2:5

WATCH SESSION 5 ON DVD

- Who is responsible for the care of our body temples?

  _____

- Who must ultimately carry out the worship, offerings, sacrifices and prayers in establishing a personal relationship with God within our body temples?

  _____

- Who is responsible for keeping the flame of love for God alive on the altar of our hearts?

  _____

- Who is responsible for keeping our consciences clear and our moral behavior free from transgression that our minds, brains and hearts be clean and clear vessels for our Lord?

  _____

- Who must be the one to initiate the process of repentance and correction of lifestyles when we err?

  _____

- Who is the one designated to take precautionary and pre-ventative measures to preserve our bodies in a healthy state and to seek appropriate remedies when repairs are needed?

  _____

- Who must be the first to take responsibility for the diagnos-ing and treatment of any illness in our bodily temples?

  _____

- Who must ultimately be the one to choose our medicines and remedies to keep our temples sound, vigorous and in good repair? _____!

PERSONAL NOTES AND "AHA!" MOMENTS

_____

_____

_____

_____

_____

_____

Discussion Questions

1. Where is the Temple in which God is located, where you can worship, and where He can be contacted?

2. How is the Temple internal to your mind and body similar to an external structural Temple?

3. What elements negatively effect or result in wear and tear on a Temple? How does aging affect your Temple?

4. Is there a cause and effect relationship between the contents of your mental Temple and your Body Temple?

5. Essential oils were a part of daily worship in the Temples of the Israelites and were responsible for maintaining a healthy environment there. What do you think about essential oils as a part of your daily life as tools, provided by God, to maintain a healthy environment in body and mind?

6. What are the consequences for not taking care of your physical Temple? Is it easy to concentrate on prayer and commune with God when your body is in pain or your mind is restless?

7. Please read again I Peter 2:5. What do you believe is the meaning of, "let yourselves be built into a spiritual house" and "be a holy priesthood"?

8. Are you ready to commit to taking better care of your body temple? What is one specific thing you are willing to commit to in this regard?

9. Are you ready to commit to keeping better care of your mind temple? Want is one specific thing you are willing to commit to in this regard?

10. As a small Bible study group, are you willing to commit to encouraging one another and to lovingly hold one another accountable?

Session 6

HEALING AND REPENTANCE

Does disease come to us as random victims of fate over which we have no control? Do people get sick through no fault of their own? Or are our maladies at least partially brought by actions of our own? And if we are at least partially at fault, then are we not then partially empowered to do something about it? If disease is not accidental, but has root causes within our minds and souls from wrong thinking, negative feelings, unhealthy habits, and improper life styles, then we do have some control. We can simply take responsibility, change the things that made us sick, and, through prayer and attunement with God's goodness, we can repent and turn back to wellness. Healing is the fruit of repentance.

We are accustomed to placing our physical, emotional, and spiritual health in the control of something or someone outside of ourselves. Our lives are thus filled with searching for solutions externally without considering that the source of our problems as well as the source of our healing is within. Do we consider that how we live our life just may be the root cause of our own illness or condition?

In this session, each of us will consider the real starting place of illness and where healing begins. We cannot help but become excited when reading of Jesus' many healings. However, this is often where many stop reading and fail to recognize the lesson in those healings that Jesus sought for you. In John 5:14, after a healing, Jesus adds the words, "Sin no more, lest a worse thing come to you." This was a powerful warning that unless the individual stopped engaging in the behaviors that caused or prolonged his illness, worse consequences could be expected. Repentance as expressed here says that you do have control over what is causing the problem. Jesus is telling us to turn away from the problem, remove the obstacles between us and God, and look to Him alone for healing with an open attitude of faith that will receive Him.

We return many times a day to the source of our illness. We replay the condition and lack of faith in God's healing power thousands of time. We feel the illness will never depart. It is no wonder we have such difficulty finding the truth about healing. Our lives have been built on the idea that we can place the blame of our condition on something or someone else. Today's lesson will allow you to fully feel how to grasp the power of prayer, the depth of God's healing resources and with clear eyes see God's healing in your own life.

It was healing and forgiveness that set Jesus apart from all other messengers. Christ not only healed the sick, the lame, and those dealing with emotional demons; He did something more! He forgave those He healed of their sins. That forgiveness restored their relationship with God. It also allowed them to forgive themselves and others. The power of forgiveness creates healing! Forgiveness is a powerful emotional experience and it can be experienced today right down to the DNA in our cells.

Christ gave specific instructions and tools for His Church to heal those who are ill and who seek God's love. Those tools and instructions are the very same today as when Christ first spoke them.

SCRIPTURE REFERENCES

The curse causeless shall not come. Proverbs 26:2

And they went out, and preached that men should repent. And they cast out many devils, and anointed with oil many that were sick, and healed them. Mark 6:12.

Purge me with hyssop, and I shall be clean: wash me, and I shall be whiter than snow . . . blot out all my iniquities. Create in me a clean heart, O God, and renew a right spirit within me. Psalm 51:3-4, 7, 9-10.

Therefore, confess your faults one to another and pray one for another, that you may be healed. James 5:16

You have been made well: Sin no more, lest a worse thing come to you. John 5:14

Forgive us our debts, as we also have forgiven our debtors. Matthew 6:12

Be merciful, just as your Father is merciful. Do not judge, and you will not be judged; do not condemn, and you will not be condemned. Forgive, and you will be forgiven; give, and it will be given to you. . . for the measure you give will be the measure you get back. Luke 6:36-38

WATCH SESSION 6 ON DVD

- The Lord's Prayer clearly states that unless we _____ others then neither can we be _____.
- In James 5 the healing mission for the elders… confessions are meant to:
- Help a person _____ their roles in creating their sicknesses
- To accept _____ for what they have done that made them sick
- To repent and _____ the habits that may have led to their health problems.
- _____ is probably the number one root of sicknesses of all kinds.
- Repentance requires _____. Repentance is a _____.
- Healing is the fruit of _____.

PERSONAL NOTES AND "AHA!" MOMENTS

_____

_____

_____

_____

_____

_____

Discussion Questions

1. Describe a time when you felt like you could never be healed.

2. When a problem appears unsolvable and yet you know a solution exists, what do you do?

3. Share your thoughts and beliefs about whether God allows healing today. Do you believe there are limits? Why or why not?

4. How do you define "repentance?" How do you interpret the meaning of the statement, "Healing is the fruit of repentance?"

5. What do you believe is the connection between emotions and illness?

6. If you could be granted one wish today with no limit or restriction, what would it be?

7. What restrictions do people place on God's healing ability? What restrictions do you find yourself placing on Him?

8. Why does God allow us to become sick?

9. Why is forgiveness so important in maintaining one's health and how is forgiveness a part of healing and repentance?

10. How can essential oils help us access and understand the roots of our illnesses and how can they assist us in our prayers for healing?

Session 7

FAITH, LOVE, PRAYER, AND OILS

The 21st century, thus far, can be defined as an age of skepticism. We are taught that, "You must prove it before you can believe it." Science is the new standard of evidence for health care and healing. This is the reality and standard most people have chosen today. The fact is that very little in our world can be evaluated or verified by this standard because application of the scientific method, powerful as it is, is narrowly restricted to only certain types of reality. When it comes to the most important spiritual realities, the opposite of what science teaches is the valid approach: "You must believe it before you can prove it." There are, in fact, types of experiments where your faith or lack of faith determines the outcome.

The fall of man (Genesis 3) brought illnesses that have continuously plagued humankind and have caused us to look for external solutions. However, when we look at history we find evidence that solutions to disease and illness have always been available to us. While we are not God, the Bible instructs us to "Be imitators of God, as beloved children, and to live in love, as Christ loved us." (Ephesians 5:1-2) It is a fact that "there is a Divinity within us," and that we can learn to express that spark of God inside by proper prayer and we can enhance that prayer by applying aromatic oils.

God's healing incense of essential oils (Exodus 30:34-36) was provided to Moses to stop a plague (Numbers 16:46-50). Leviticus 14 discusses yet another blend of oils (Hyssop and Cedarwood) that God provided to Moses for a variety of healing applications. Jesus gives us specific instructions on the kind of prayer that is effective and gets results as well as insight on why some forms of prayer are not effective. We also learn that when we pray for healing, God's answer is usually not by way of an instant miracle, but by way of a gradual healing which may take hours, days, weeks, or months. We also learn that in their healing ministries, gradual healing (not miracles) was the experience of the disciples most of the time. This fact makes it easier to engage in a healing ministry ourselves because we realize that God does not expect us to perform miracles, but only to facilitate healing however long it takes. We can all do that.

This material can be compared to finding a very precious treasure you put away long ago in a chest for safekeeping and then forgot you even had it. Dr. Stewart helps dust off our Biblical chest, showing us how the power of prayer and aromatic oils work to reinforce one another, reaching to the very foundation of life within our cells, giving us the ability to defend ourselves against disease.

SCRIPTURE REFERENCES

The Lord said to Moses: Take sweet spices, stacte (myrrh), and onycha, and galbanum, these sweet spices with pure frankincense (an equal part of each), and you shall make an incense blended as by the perfumer, seasoned with salt, pure and holy; and you shall beat some of it into a powder, and put part of it before the covenant in the tent of meeting where I shall meet with you: It shall be for you most holy. Exodus 30: 34-36.

Ask, and it will be given you; search, and you will find; knock, and the door will be opened for you. For everyone who asks receives, and everyone who searches finds, and for everyone who knocks, the door will be opened. Matthew 7:7-8

You do not have, because you do not ask. You ask and do not receive, because you ask wrongly. James 4:2-3

If you, then, who are evil, know how to give good gifts to your children, how much more will the heavenly Father give the Holy Spirit to those who ask him! Luke 11:13

Will not God grant justice to his chosen ones who cry to him day and night? Will he delay long in helping them? I tell you, he will quickly grant justice to them. Luke 18:7

Jesus said to him, "If you are able! All things can be done for the one who believes." Immediately the father of the child cried out, "I believe; help thou my unbelief." Mark 9:23-24

The Lord is near. Do not worry about anything, but in everything by prayer and supplication with thanksgiving let your requests be made known to God. Philippians 4:5-6

This is the boldness that we have in him, that if we ask anything according to his will, he hears us. And if we know that he hears us in whatever we ask, we know that we have obtained the requests made of him. I John 5:14–15

Very truly, I tell you, the one who believes in me will also do the works that I do and, in fact, will do greater works than these. John 14:12

Love never ends. . . as for prophecies, they will come to an end; . . . as for knowledge, it will come to an end. For we know only in part, and we prophesy only in part. . . for now we see in a mirror, dimly, but then we will see face to face. . . now faith, hope, and love abide, these three; and the greatest of these is love. I Corinthians 13:8–13

WATCH SESSION 7 ON DVD

Why do you think it often takes time for prayers to be answered? Jesus performed many miracles where healings were instant or within minutes. Why can't we get the same results? Jesus said we would do His works, and even greater works.

Three words for healing:
- _____ – "instant, miraculous healing"
- _____ – "deliverance or salvation"
- _____ – "gradual healing with menial service or care
- God wants us to be _____.
- _____ is the channel through which God's healing grace most easily flows.
- God is _____. The power that heals is none other than Love itself.

PERSONAL NOTES AND "AHA!" MOMENTS

_____

_____

_____

_____

_____

_____

Discussion Questions

1. What do you believe is the scientific standard? Can you
    think of any situation where the scientific method would not
    be able to verify, evaluate, or ascertain the truth?

2. What kind of proof do we demand from God before we
    will believe?

3. James 4:3 says that when we pray, if we ask and receive not, it
    is because we "ask amiss" or "ask wrongly." What are some of
    the things we could be doing in our praying for healing that
    are "amiss" or "wrong" that results in a prayer unanswered?

4. What is prayer to you? What are some of the attributes of ef-
    fective prayer, as given in the Scriptures?

5. Be honest, have you ever prayed for someone's healing and
    he or she did not get better? What effect did this have on
    your relationship with God?

6. Were all of the healings mentioned in the New Testament
    instant and miraculous? Does God ask us to do miracles?
    Or does He expect a different kind of healing ministry
    from us? Would this healing ministry be any different than
    that of His disciples?

7. How can science, oil, prayer, and faith work together?

8. Do you ever doubt God's ability and, if so, when do you
    most doubt God's ability?

9. What potential health problems do you think God antici-
    pated that mankind would create for Himself?

10. List all of the things about God and prayer that you know
    with a certainty in your heart. How can you use these cer-
    tainties to strengthen your faith in areas where you are not
    yet so sure?

Session 8

THE GREAT COMMISSION AND BEYOND

A Sunday School teacher once compared the Great Commission (Matthew 28:19) to a phrase in an old television show: "If you choose to accept this mission." The choice is still the same. If you choose to accept this mission your life will forever be changed.

The Scriptures tell us in Acts 10:38 that Jesus was anointed by God with the power of the Holy Spirit to heal those who were oppressed by the devil.

In the 21st century we seek out solutions to man's greatest health challenges by using the best that science has to offer. However, today's advances in healthcare have not made life disease-free; instead our society is plagued by resilient virulent viruses, monster bacteria that resist all known antibiotics, along with increasing numbers of children with learning disabilities, people on life-time prescriptions of antidepressant drugs, and others with persistent mental health challenges. People acknowledge they have prayed to God and nothing happened. They say, "God did not hear me or heal me; I am still sick."

The truth is we often look to science for answers when science does not have the answers. There are spiritual healing tools that we know can work by faith, but can science prove they are factual? We should all be asking ourselves what is really going on in our world.

As we conclude our study we see how science and faith work together. Science now allows us to learn the secrets behind one of God's greatest gifts: essential oils created directly by His Divine Majesty, Himself! Oils imbued with His Word. Oils impregnated with His intelligence.

This Session brings us to the culmination of how science, beliefs, faith, prayer, love, and anointing, through the power of the Holy Spirit, can bring about healing. There is something special to be learned by those who use, "the effectual fervent prayer" (James 5:14-16) that truly has the capacity to heal our greatest illnesses. There are no limits to God's healing power.

Remember, God's will is not to heal you; God's good and perfect will is for you to not become sick in the first place! We may view that as impossible, but it truly is possible for God!

SCRIPTURE REFERENCES

Go you therefore, and teach all nations, baptizing them in the name of the Father and of the Son, and of the Holy Ghost: Teaching them to observe all things whatsoever I have commanded you. Matthew 28:19-20

And he called to Him the twelve and began to send them forth by two and two; and gave them power over unclean spirits . . .And they cast out many devils, and anointed with oil many that were sick, and healed them. Mark 6:7, 13

After these things the Lord appointed other seventy also, and sent them two and two before His face into every city and place, where He Himself would come. Therefore said He to them, . . . into whatsoever city you enter, and they receive you, eat such things as are set before you: And heal the sick that are therein, and say to them, 'The kingdom of God is come near to you.'. . . And the seventy returned with joy, saying, "Lord in your name even the demons submit to us!" Luke 10:1-2, 8-9, 17

Go unto all the world and proclaim the good news to the whole creation. . . And these signs will accompany those who believe: by using my name they will cast out demons. . . they will lay their hands on the sick, and they will recover. Mark 16:15, 17-18

Is any sick among you? Let him call for the elders of the church; and let them pray over him, anointing him with oil in the name of the Lord: And the prayer of faith shall save the sick, and the Lord shall raise him up; and if he have committed sins, they shall be forgiven him. Confess your faults one to another and pray one for another, that you may be healed. The effectual fervent prayer of a righteous man avails much. James 5:14-16

If you do not doubt in your heart, but believe that what you say will come to pass, it will be done for you. So I tell you, whatever you ask for in prayer believe that you have received it, and it will be yours. Mark 11:23-24

And now, Lord, . . . grant to your servants to speak your word with all boldness, while you stretch out your hand to heal, and signs and wonders are performed through the name of your holy servant, Jesus. Acts 4:29-30

You are a chosen race, a royal priesthood, a holy nation, God's own people, in order that you may proclaim the mighty acts of him who called you out of darkness into his marvelous light. I Peter 2:9

WATCH SESSION 8 ON DVD

Were the Great Commissions expressed in the New Testament only for those living at the time of Christ? Were they to be limited to baptizing and preaching, as expressed at the end of Matthew, or were other Commissions, such as healing, also implied and expressed by Christ Himself?

- God's _____ were not only for those living at the time of Christ.
- Jesus also commissioned His followers to:
  - _____
  - _____
  - _____
  - _____
- We must _____ given to us.
- We must _____ that God clearly reveals His mission for us.
- You are _____ and the gift of _____ is yours for the asking if you are willing to develop it by diligent and devotional effort with prayer and sincerity.

PERSONAL NOTES AND "AHA!" MOMENTS

_____

_____

_____

_____

_____

_____

Discussion Questions

1. What do you now know about anointing?

2. What, in your opinion, is the difference between a person
    with a demon and a person with mental illness?

3. If you were healed by spiritual means could you keep it
    a secret?

4. You now have the gift of healing, if you choose to accept it.
    What would you do with this ability first?

5. There are successful healing ministries that use prayer only and do well without applying essential oils. Do you think these ministries would have even greater healing success by incorporating oils?

6. There are successful aromatherapy practices that use oils only and do well without engaging in prayer. Do you think these practices would have even greater healing success by incorporating prayer?

7. What part does belief or faith play in healing? What do you believe is the difference between "faith" and "beliefs"?

8. Would the elders of your church know what to do if sick members were to seek them out for prayer, laying on of hands, anointing with oil, and to hear their confessions, as described in James 5:14-17?

9. Who in your life is now sick? Share a time you spoke a prayer of faith for yourself or someone you love.

10. We have a population that has no references to any healing but modern medicine. What can we tell them now about oils, prayer and healing? Can we be confident that these are effective spiritual alternatives to material medical means for the treatment of disease?

11. Would you be willing to lead a group through this lesson series? If so, where and when would you start?

SHARE YOUR STORY – If you would like to share a testimony of your own healing, you may do this under "Share Your Story" at www.godsforgottengift.com.

Small Group Leader Guide

An exciting opportunity lies ahead. Our goal is to equip you, the small group leader, with as much information as possible to lead a successful and rewarding study. Over the course of this study your group will be discovering Scriptures in a way they may have never before considered. You are about to guide a group of people seeking wisdom, solutions, and possibilities for their life. When someone is looking for spiritual solutions, the Bible is often the resource of choice. *Healing: God's Forgotten Gift* will not only extend the understanding of spiritual health but will also offer insight into how God seeks to heal each of our lives in all areas; often in miraculous ways! In order to receive the most out of this study, we are asking for each leader to pray for and expect a miracle to occur somewhere in your group. What type of miracle? Only God can decide. We are only to pray and believe it will happen!

Group Session Guide

THIS STUDY IS NOT ABOUT YOU! As the group leader you do not need to have all the answers. Isn't that a relief? The Scriptures, video teaching and study material will provide many opportunities for enlightenment. Your role is to guide a group of people through a time of learning, discovery and discussion. It will be helpful for you to take on the mindset of magnifying God and minimizing yourself. The more you learn about all that God has provided for us the more you will take on the hints of John the Baptist, "He must increase, but I must decrease" (John 3:30). Your position as the group leader is simply to co-labor with God to bless everyone in the group.

The other side of this first helpful tip is leaders are most successful when you make the study all about God and the healing gifts He has provided. The best leader is one who is first a follower. Ask Him to empower you with wisdom beyond your abilities, and return to prayer often. By opening and closing each session with prayer you are putting God at the center of each session.

The leader's emotional place will set the emotional tone for your session. Adopt a joyful and celebratory attitude throughout the study. Your attitude will become infectious with joy and love that will significantly improve the entire group's study experience.

You may not know this but joy does not just happen. It's something you cannot engineer on demand and you cannot pretend to be joyful for long. Real joy starts with seeing clearly the opportunity God has placed before you. God has blessed you by allowing you to lead this group. This reflection leads to gratitude for the opportunity, and out of gratitude flows joy, both in your preparation and in your discussion.

Housekeeping Tips for a successful small group experience:

- Make sure everyone in the group has their own copy of the study guide. This will be helpful for following along with the video teaching which has room for taking notes, along with a few other resources we have provided to make the most of your small group experience. The Scriptures for each session are printed in the study guide. Those who choose to bring their own Bibles are encouraged to do so. Throughout the study they may want to make notes, underline or highlight verses to come back to during their personal study time.

- Hold weekly meetings with a consistent starting and ending time agreed upon by the group. Bi-monthly meetings will work, but our experience is the group bonds quicker and the materials stay fresh if you commit to weekly meetings.

- When your meeting time begins, allow for a brief connection time each week, usually about 10 - 15 minutes, discussing personal celebrations, discoveries and wins for the week.

- Open the study time with prayer. As a group (taking turns reading aloud encourages participation, but don't force it) read the opening paragraphs and the accompanying Scripture references before watching Dr. Stewart's video teaching. Each teaching segment will take approximately 20 minutes.

- You will gain the most from this study if you, the leader, give yourself some time to prepare in advance. We suggest watching the video teaching and reading through the Scriptures at least a day ahead of time. This will give you some time to reflect on the material as well as look up any additional resources you might want to use. These can be found at www.godsforgottengift.com.

- Guide the group discussion - keeping this to 30 - 45 minutes.

- End the study time with prayer requests. Allow those willing to pray out loud to do so. Encourage them as the weeks go along. For many this is uncomfortable. Share with them this is a time to talk to God, not judge one another's words. Share with your group that a sentence or two from a person's heart is pleasing and acceptable to God.

- Dismiss at the agreed upon time. Be respectful of people's time.

More tips for a successful small group experience:

Encourage accountability

Accountability matters, and by seeing that it does matter causes a direct effect upon ones life. We're more likely to experience permanent change when we have an accountability partner who will support each other. Ask the group to partner up, men with men and women with women, during the week. This helps hold each other accountable and gives them an opportunity to share enlightenments, thoughts and what God is doing in their lives. This can be done over coffee, email or a text message. This isn't meant to be a legalistic tool; simply an opportunity to gain the most from the study time.

Preparation

Preparation will help you create a map for each session. Dr. Stewart will provide all the teaching. It will prove most helpful to you and your group if you watch the teaching ahead of time, read through the Scriptures and discussion questions, familiarizing yourself with the material. All you need to do is prepare by knowing what the others may not know and what to expect. It will be a very valuable tool to have an idea of approximately how much time you can give each question.

Create a safe environment for sharing

New people coming to a small group for the first time often come with lots of past baggage and fears. Take it slow and realize people are easily intimidated and shy. There is something special about coming to a place and feeling safe, honored, and valued. Achieving that is not as difficult as it sounds. What it takes is the ability to tell the group from the beginning, "What is said in group stays in group." And mean that with all your heart. Value individual feelings even when you disagree. Some of the teachings will stretch even the most mature Christian. There may come a time when it's appropriate to raise and examine differences. When this happens, be as loving and valuing to all individuals as possible. It may be best to encourage those involved to "agree to disagree" and wait until the group has begun to mature and grow in strength. As the weeks go on you will find group members discovering and growing in their relationship with God and one another. New discoveries about themselves and all relationships in their lives will give them a greater appreciation for the diversity of God's creation and love for one another.

The power of listening

Focus on what each person is saying, rather than what you may think they are thinking. Give yourself time to rephrase the question if need be rather than what you are going to respond with. Learn to listen with your HEART and not your intellect.

Be sure to review the Scripture readings

Scripture is the filter for this whole session. Each session will have Scriptures to review and think over. Many of these Scripture verses will appear new to the group members. The Scriptures are not new. They have simply been glanced over for many years.

Smoothly moving conversation and questions

It's invaluable to always know where you want to go next with your group discussion. Sometimes you may need to announce the transition, for example, "let's turn a corner now and look at the next question." The group experience flows more smoothly if you capitalize on natural transition points. Simply listen for comments that move the discussion forward.

Echo what has been said

This is a very powerful and simple leader technique. You will find it helpful from time to time to restate what someone has said—to "repeat or echo" it for the group. It will help that group member feel their point has been understood and valued. It also adds value by allowing time for other members of the group to gather their own thoughts and add it to the conversation. Invite commentary on what was said as the flow of the conversation improves.

Connecting the information to daily life

Connecting a piece of information with what someone else shared earlier will help everyone gain a clearer understanding of the Scriptures, comments, video teaching, as well as one another.

What to expect in your Group

In every group there are individuals who are shy and reserved; some will share openly, and still others may not say anything. This does not mean they are not experiencing the material or not moved by God's Word. Sometimes you may see the person has something they want to share but they won't jump into the discussion. It may be helpful if you look to the person and ask, "_____, you look deep in thought. Is there something you would like to share?" This gives them an opportunity to contribute without interrupting. If they choose not to, that's okay. You may want to have a conversation in private. Some may be reflecting inwardly and not want to share with the group at this point.

Many groups will be blessed with a spirited person who contributes a little too much. Excessive contribution by one individual can disturb the experience for the whole group. As the leader you will need to be in control and guide the group along in discussion. The best way to get the most from the powerful contributor and smoothly maintain leadership is to start by affirming the positive and then candidly make your request, "Lori, you really have a lot of good stuff to add to the study, and I want to ensure that the rest of the group has an adequate opportunity to add value."

A second way to balance contribution is to simply cut in when the dominator takes a breath, echo what he or she has said to the point and invite additional responses.

Ask for their thoughts and getting the group to talk

Sample questions might include: "How about someone that has not spoken yet?" "Anyone else care to comment?" "How about a different perspective?" "What do you think of the question?"

After individuals have shared, thank them for sharing. You want everyone to feel valued, loved and supported. This encourages them to share, if they feel valued, loved and safe to do so.

The greatest challenge is to know when to "Not Speak"

A group leader's most challenging job is to know when to keep silent. Ask the question that is provided for you or you can create your own open-ended question. Never be uncomfortable with silence. Sometimes it simply takes a few moments for people to process mentally all they have heard and how to begin to use it in their life. How they create ways to use God's tools will be fascinating to watch unfold. Learn how to effectively use patience when silence occurs.

For group leaders who are especially time-conscious, it's natural to want to march through a set of questions to make sure everything gets covered in the time allotted. The best group leaders, however, remain mindful that the real goal of the group is to experience God's word, love and transformation in our lives, not completing the material. A life-changing group experience comes when everyone feels time has been given to share with one another in the context of God's word being applied to their lives.

Dealing with the unexpected

No matter how much information this study guide provides you, nothing will prepare you more than a humble prayerful heart. God will provide you with exactly what you need in order to lead. Your greatest asset is your willingness to be vulnerable and authentic. A great small group experience not only involves good Bible study but also involves relationships where we can be real with each other. This study offers a rare opportunity to be a part of healing, not just physically, emotionally and spiritually, but also of relationships. If pain arises surrounding an event by one of the group members, be empathic and nonjudgmental. Expect real healing to occur and uplift them with God's love and prayer.

Healing

One gets the impression from reading the Scriptures that Jesus and/or his disciples healed people instantly every time. That is not so. There are three Greek words translated as "healing" in the New Testament, all with a different meaning:

1. *Iaomai*—means miraculous or instantaneous and is found 30 times in the New Testament.

2. *Therapeuo*-which means therapy, is found 40 times. Therapeuo means, literally, "to serve, to attend to, or to wait upon menially," or in other words, "to heal gradually over time with care."

3. *Sozo*—is found only three times and implies not only a physical healing but an emotional and spiritual healing as well. Literally, sozo means "to become sound or whole," in mind body and spirit.

Resources and additional books

Additional resources are available at www.godsforgottengift.com.

Planning steps for connections to multiple groups in one church

This study is designed so you can play Dr. Stewart's teaching video to a large group and then break into smaller groups for discussion time. Alternatively, the teaching fits well in a small group in someone's home. Either way is effective.

Flyer for starting your group (advertising ideas for starting your small group)

Go to www.godsforgottengift.com for flyers that can be edited and printed to promote your small group.

Promoting your study

- Word of mouth, inviting a friend, co-worker or acquaintance is the best form of advertising.

- If your organization, church, or worship facility is planning this study as a large group/small group course, public advertising can be done, taking registrations in advance of the study. Prior to the first meeting, prayerfully place individuals into small groups for their discussion time. It is best if these groups stay the same over the course of the eight-week sessions.

- Bulletin or worship folder announcements can be made; social networking sites inviting your friends, email invites. Anything to get the word out about your upcoming study will be beneficial. Your enthusiasm is contagious, so spread the word!

leader's notes

Session 1
GOD'S GIFT FROM THE BEGINNING

GOALS:

- To help you realize that it is a good thing to desire to be a healer through Christ, just as His disciples and the Christians of the early church were healers.

- That it is possible for you to become a healer.

- Become familiar with the Scriptures that express how God's love is such, that even before He created Adam and Eve, He was looking ahead to a time when we, His children would need medicines and the ability to heal one another.

- How, out of God's love, He gave us herbs and plant oils as medicines and instilled us with His attributes, including the Gift of Healing.

HEALTH ASSESSMENT TOOL

Before you begin any of the study this week, have everyone take a few moments to fill out the Health Assessment Tool in the back of your study guide. Don't over think the questions, have fun with it. Score it and then begin the study. We will return to the assessment at the end of the series to see how everyone has progressed over the eight weeks.

KEY POINTS FROM SCRIPTURE

1. God put His first people in a garden, not in a house.

2. God gave us plants, with their leaves and the oils of their
    leaves, for medicines.

3. God created us in His image, i.e. with His attributes.

4. The Scriptures instruct us to earnestly desire God's best gifts.

5. The Gift of Healing is a Divine attribute, a spiritual gift God
    wants us to receive and share.

ADDITIONAL SCRIPTURES IN DVD TEACHING

From time to time Dr. Stewart references other Scriptures that he
did not have the group read before the teaching time. When this
happens, we will provide a listing of those references for your con-
venience. It is up to you and your group members as to whether you
wish to look those up for additional study. Matthew 7:10; Luke 11:10

A NOTE TO THE HOST:

We begin this study at the beginning of God's Word in the book
of Genesis. If you are unfamiliar with the creation story, take a
few moments and read through the first chapter of Genesis. We
will be focusing on only a few of these verses, but it will help give
you some context into the basis of the entire study. Each week
when your group comes together, open with prayer and then
have the group members read through the opening paragraphs
in the Study Guide. Encourage everyone to take turns reading aloud, however, some may not be comfortable doing so.
That's okay. You don't want to make anyone uncomfortable. It's

more important they hear the Word of God than to participate in reading anything out loud. Then read through each of the Scripture verses before watching Dr. Stewart's teaching. Make sure each participant has a pen or pencil to fill in blanks and take notes. Encourage everyone to bring their own Bible to each session, as they may want to make notations in it.

All the questions this week are intended to be very open ended, allowing everyone an opportunity to share what they think or something they gleaned from Dr. Stewart's teachings. There are no right or wrong answers. As the group comes together and begins this journey, encourage everyone to share, but do not force it.

WRAP UP: In the coming weeks we will focus more on God's provisions and the gift of healing. Close your time together with prayer, asking for God's miraculous healing to take place in each of the participant's lives and to expect a miracle either spoken or unspoken. The Lord knows the personal needs of each one and only He can bring healing to our lives. Encourage everyone who wants to pray to do so; no pressure for those who choose not to. Thank everyone for coming and sharing. Now would be a good time to encourage everyone to invite a friend to next week's study.

GIFTS DISCUSSED IN SESSION 1

VALOR ®

(A blend of oils containing Sweet Almond, Spruce, Rosewood, Blue Tansy, Frankincense)

Historical uses:

- Place on the bottom of feet to self-correct spine
- Balance the body electrical energies
- Enhances spiritual well being
- Apathy
- Restlessness
- Sadness
- Sciatica
- Self-esteem
- Shock
- Supports endocrine system
- Apnea
- Back pain
- Herniated disk
- Feeling betrayed
- Muscle pain
- Depression
- Broken heel
- Courage
- Overcoming fear

JOY™

This blend contains several uplifting oils in use during Biblical times. These include rosewood, jasmine, roman chamomile and rose. Joy also contains oil not known to be used in Biblical times. These include bergamot, mandarin, lemon, ylang ylang, geranium and palmarosa.

Historical uses:

- Apathy
- Argumentative emotionally
- Cancer
- Depression
- Deodorant
- Sadness
- Despair
- Disappointments
- Balance emotions
- Mood swings
- Stress

leader's notes

Session 2

OILS AND HEALING

GOALS:

- To encourage you to consider when Jesus called the twelve and sent them out to heal the sick and appointed seventy others to do likewise, His commission to heal extends down through the ages to us today.

- To realize that in our healing mission we are to be selective upon whom we apply our healing intentions and upon whom not.

- To understand not everyone is a qualified candidate for spiritual healing.

KEY POINTS FROM SCRIPTURE

1. Those whom Jesus sent forth to heal were instilled with power over "unclean spirits," meaning all forms of sickness, mental, emotional, physical and, including, actual demonic possessions.

2. In addition to the twelve, Jesus commissioned many others to travel from town to town healing the sick.

3. Only those who gave some indication of their willingness to receive healing were healed.

4. Anointing with oil was part of the means of healing taught by Jesus to the followers He dispatched for such missions.

ADDITIONAL SCRIPTURES IN DVD TEACHING

Mark 3:1-5; Luke 13:10-13; John 5:6-8, 11:1-3, 43-44; Exodus 30:22-25, 34-36; Number 16:46-50; Mark 6:11; Luke 10:10

If you or group members are unfamiliar with these healings Jesus performed, the group can read through them if time allows, or share them with group members to read at home. The references Dr. Stewart makes from Exodus, Numbers and Leviticus will be studied more in depth next week.

A NOTE FOR HOSTS:

As Dr. Stewart closes his teaching today, he mentions that the intelligent and informed application of healing oils, combined with prayer, physical touch and loving assistance can help people bring to memory, uncover, confess and release the buried emotions that may have caused or contributed to their illness. This may bring some face-to-face with a reality they had never considered before. You will want to take the time to work through this study yourself and perhaps seek additional resources on www.godsforgottengift.com. More of this will be covered in Session 6. If this does not come up in this week's session, please prepare yourself in the weeks ahead by allowing enough time to preview Dr. Stewart's teachings and seeking God's wisdom through additional prayer time.

QUESTION 1. The emphasis on this question is "as you requested." God always answers our prayers in one of three ways: yes, no, wait. Therefore, the answer may not be quite what we thought it would be.

QUESTION 6. We are beginning to touch on how emotions can contribute to illness in the body. We have all seen or experienced the effects of stress and other negative emotions. Dr. Stewart will explore this further in Session 6.

QUESTION 7. "Poor self worth" is not humility. Some are of the belief that they must have a poor self worth in order to be humble in the eyes of God. Everyone is a child of God, created by Him; therefore each of us is of great value and precious to God.

QUESTION 10. Jesus instructed His disciples, and us, that we are to walk away from those who reject us. This is very hard to do. Share with the group Jesus' words written in Luke 10:16.

WRAP UP: Close group discussion in prayer thanking God for the teaching and discussion time. Allow everyone who desires to pray to do so. Praise God for revealing Himself to us in His Word. Let the healing power of Christ flow through you as you come together as a group. Love and care for those who may need an extra measure of God's grace.

GIFTS DISCUSSED IN SESSION 2

FRANKINCENSE

(*Boswellia carterii*)

Historical Uses:

- Used to treat every ailment of man.
- Considered the "Holy anointing oil."
- Used to create spiritual awareness.
- Used for respiratory infections.
- Used for inflammation.
- Used on insect bites to help reduce swelling and speed healing.
- Applied on back of neck to help improve concentration
- Added to honey or milk and ingested daily for health maintenance.
- Diluted 50/50 with extra virgin olive oil and apply to a blistered area of burns.
- Diffused or inhale from the bottle to help with mood elevation.
- Burned in the temple for spiritual connection and uplifting of emotions.
- Used for help with insomnia.
- Applied to nails to help strengthen brittle or weak nails.
- Used to soften skin.
- Helped reduce and remove tumors, warts, and moles.

MYRRH

(*Commiphora myrrha*)

Historical Uses:

- Used to promote spiritual awareness.
- Used to remove stretch marks on women and soften skin.
- Diffused to help with childbirth.
- Used as an anti-inflammatory.
- Known for its antiviral capabilities.
- Calming effect during periods of stress.
- Helped canker sores disappear.
- One to two drops on gums has helped heal gingivitis.
- Two to five drops in water for an excellent mouthwash.
- Placed 1 drop on a blemish to help it go away.

leader's notes

Session 3

OILS FOR SPIRITUAL PURPOSES

GOALS:

- To help you understand that the Holy Anointing Oil and the Holy Incense given in Exodus for the Israelites to use in their place of worship were not only for spiritual purposes to facilitate prayer and meditation, they were also the antibacterial agents by which God protected His people from infectious disease.

- To understand God's thoughtfulness in protecting the Old Testament people from disease with essential oils still applies to us today.

KEY POINTS FROM SCRIPTURE:

1. Anointing with oil is a practice prescribed by God, Himself.

2. Modern science has discovered that the aromatic ingredients of the Holy Anointing Oil are all highly antiseptic, effective against harmful bacteria, viruses, parasites, and fungi.

3. The scriptures in Exodus 30 instruct Moses that not only are the sons of Aaron (priests of the temple) to be anointed, but everything on and around the altar of burnt offering.

4. Exodus 30* also offers a God-given recipe for a Holy Incense to be diffused continuously in the tabernacle. This Incense is also highly antimicrobial against all sorts of pathogenic bacteria, viruses, parasites, and fungi. (*In this session we have participants reading through verse 36. Verses 37-38 contain prohibitions against these oils for use outside the Temple or with "strangers." Some people have expressed fears of committing an offense against God if the Holy Anointing Oil or Holy Incense were actually used today. If such a conversation or concern should come up in your group, please refer to Jeremiah 31:31-34, which addresses the New Covenant as superseding the Old. An appropriate response is also available in *Healing Oils of the Bible* (pp. 68-69) or can be found on www. godsforgottengift.com.)

ADDITIONAL SCRIPTURES IN DVD TEACHING

Psalm 133; John 12:3; Numbers 16:46-50
These are provided in the event you choose to do further reading or group members want to read them together or at home.

QUESTION 2. Colic, dysentery, hoof and mouth disease, yellow fever, plagues and more.

QUESTION 3. Rebellion and rejection.

QUESTION 4. Holy anointing oil and Holy incense.

QUESTION 6. Show yourself.

QUESTION 7. Remember, give people time to think of something.

WRAP UP: Close in prayer thanking God for being in the details of our lives! Thank Him for the teachings He has already provided and the ones He is revealing to us through this study. Encourage everyone to pray a one-sentence prayer of thanks for a detail God provided for them in their lives. Thank everyone for sharing in the study time today.

GIFTS DISCUSSED IN SESSION 3

ALOES/SANDALWOOD

(*Santalum album*)

Historical Use:

- Used as a skin preservative.
- Soften kink and remove wrinkles.
- Used to enhance deep sleep.
- Applied on tumors to remove them.
- Rubbed above the eyebrows around the eye 1-3 times daily to help with vision.
- Used as men's perfume and cologne.
- Used in bath water to disperse or combine with bath salts for a relaxing bath.

- Applied on tummy area for acute or chronic diarrhea.
- Apply one drop to a cold sore.
- Massaged in hair and on scalp to retard graying.
- Used to prevent infection from wounds and to speed wound healing.

3 WISE MEN™

(A blend of oils containing Sandalwood (Aloes), Myrrh, Juniper, Frankincense, Spruce, and Almond Oil as a base)

Historical Use:

- Colitis
- Emotional Trauma
- Bacterial infections
- Mucus
- Shock
- Skin ulcers
- Throat infections
- Yeast infections
- Balance emotions

GALBANUM (Ferula gummosa)

Historical uses:

- Used in the temple to bring feelings back into emotional balance.
- Used for that time of the month when a woman needs a little up lifting or was cramping.
- Used for indigestion by putting a drop on the outside of the stomach.
- Used during times of prayer for a deeper spiritual awareness by applying to the bottom of the feet and applying a drop in

hands, then rubbing hands together, cupping over nose and
breathing deeply.
- When combined with frankincense brought a spiritual uplifting.
- Inhaled or applied to temples or massage into scalp to
relieve a headache.

Exodus II™

(A blend of oils containing Cassia, Hyssop, Frankincense,
Spikenard, Galbanum, Myrrh, Cinnamon Bark, and Calamus
in a carrier of Olive Oil)

Historical uses:

· Anthrax	· Influence
· Bacterial infection	· Hepatitis
· Blisters	· Bronchitis
· Boils blisters	· Pneumonia
· Breathing problems	· Gingivitis
· Colds	· Bacterial infection
· Cramps	· Viral infection
· Emphysema	· Sleep disorder
· Grief	· Seizures
· Nausea	· Plagues

leader's notes

Session 4

CEDARWOOD AND SOLOMON

GOALS:

- To recognize the special properties of cedarwood oil as presented in the Bible.

- Recognize that inhaling cedarwood in their living environment was mentally enhancing, conducive to prayer and meditation, and emotionally releasing.

- Recognize that cedarwood was an oil of preservation and protection.

- Recognize that it was an oil for healing a variety of diseases in Biblical times.

- To see applications for cedarwood oil in our lives today.

KEY POINTS FROM SCRIPTURE:

1. The cedars of Lebanon were special, considered as sacred "Trees of the Lord."

2. Cedarwood oil, combined with Hyssop oil, was applied as a cleansing ritual for any "leprous disease" appearing as rashes, lesions, eruptions, swellings, or scabs on the skin, as well as for bona fide cases of leprosy itself.

3. The bodily locations for anointing with oil given in Leviticus for "leprous diseases" are very specific, each of which have specific emotional implications.

4. A house or temple made of cedarwood would continuously exude the fragrance of cedar, serving as a stimulant to the mind, a scent that brings a sense of peace, as well as a protection from decay and the onslaught of insects, microbes, and gnawing rodents.

ADDITIONAL SCRIPTURES IN DVD TEACHING

Genesis 50:26. You may want to read through the scriptures in the opening paragraphs before group time to give a historical context.

QUESTION 7. Solomon was glorifying God by using the very best building materials and one with aromatic benefit allowed him to govern the kingdom and God's people to the very best of His ability.

WRAP UP: Encourage group members to share prayers with God in your group setting. By now some should become more comfortable praying (talking to God) in the group. Encourage praise reports for the healing that is taking place, physically, emotionally and spiritually. Thank God for all He has shown your group in these past four weeks and the growth each member has experienced!

GIFTS DISCUSSED IN SESSION 4

CEDARWOOD

(*Cedrus atlantica*)

Historical uses:

- Diffused or inhaled to enhance prayer, meditation and mental clarity.
- Applied on location as an effective insect repellant.
- Repelled insects and keeps clothing fragrant and smelling fresh.
- Applied a drop or two to the soles of the feet to enhance the immune system and boost the body's natural defenses.
- Rubbed into the scalp to possibly inhibit hair loss.
- Used on wounds on the skin to help clean, disinfect and protect from infection.
- Rubbed on the chest area either diluted or full strength to help relieve symptoms of congestion.
- Enhanced deep sleep when inhaled directly from the bottle or a drop applied near the temples and the back of the neck.

leader's notes

Session 5

OILS, TEMPLE MAINTENANCE AND REPAIR

GOALS:

- For you to realize where God is to be sought while living in a physical form, which is within the temple of our personal bodies and within our hearts and minds.

- To help you realize that taking care of God's temple means following God's laws of emotional, mental, and physical health. This means taking proper measures to feed our bodies with proper nutrition and exercise, to feed our minds with uplifting thoughts, such as those found in scripture and sung in praise songs, and to feed our hearts with love, humility, patience, kindness, gratitude, and hope.

KEY POINTS FROM SCRIPTURE:

1. The Temple within which we all must find God is our body.

2. God's presence is within ourselves.

3. It is God's wish that we be in good health, both physical and mental.

4. It is our duty and responsibility to build, maintain, and repair our body Temples.

5. It is also our duty to keep our mind Temples clean and filled with thoughts of God.

WRAP UP: Close in prayer, encouraging the group to thank God for the physical Temple He has created in our bodies. Ask for forgiveness for not caring for our Temples as He would have us. Invite Him in to do a cleansing in your Temple that would be suitable for Him to reside. Thank God for the teaching He has given.

Don't Forget! Discuss what type of celebration your group might like to have as suggested in the Help for Hosts video. Set the date and allow everyone to find a role to fill so the entire group is sharing in creating this fun event.

GIFTS DISCUSSED IN SESSION 5

CASSIA

(*Cinnamomum cassia*)

Historical Use:
- Used as part of oil for anointing.
- Diffused or a drop placed in the hand, rub hands together and cupped over the nose for a joyful, uplifting feeling.
- Add a drop to water, then swish in the mouth and gargle for an effective mouthwash.
- Used in cooking, for example, add a drop or two to yams.

- Diluted 50/50 with extra virgin olive oil and applied to area of concern helped with boils, ringworm, and fungal infections.
- Combined with carrier oil and other oils such as Frankincense, Sandalwood, Myrrh, Hyssop, or Galbanum and worn as a fragrance.
- Put a drop in a glass of water and shake it up (to disperse the oil) for a protecting & refreshing drink. May alleviate sugar cravings!
- Taken internally to help with fungal problems!
- Rub one drop on the outside of an apple and eat to help boost immune system.

MYRTLE

(*Myrtus communis*)

Historical Use:

- Applied on the thyroid and to balance hypothyroidism and normalize thyroid. Mix with a bit of carrier oil and apply to base of neck just under the Adam's apple.
- Rubbed on bronchioles for bronchitis. Used in the shower at first sign of attack.
- For a cough added one drop in a teaspoon of honey.
- For a chronic cough, diffused, applied to throat and chest area.
- Used for diarrhea, by rubbing on stomach.
- Used for prostate decongestant by applying a drop or two to inside ankle and heel.
- Used for children's coughs and chest complaints as this is a relatively mild essential oil. May dilute with extra virgin olive oil before applying to child's throat and chest.

ONYCHA

(*Styrax benzoin*)

Historical Use:

- Placed a drop on a cut or scrape to speed healing and help prevent infection.
- Placed a drop on a wound to help slow bleeding.
- Placed a drop on each underarm instead of deodorant.
- Diluted 1 drop in a teaspoon of honey or 4 oz. of rice milk and ingested to help with a cold, cough or sore throat.
- Rubbed several drops on the stomach to help ease gripping pains of cramps.

CYPRESS

(*Cupressus sempervirens*)

Historical uses:

- Used as a deodorant.
- Used for arthritis discomfort.
- Used to ease cramping.
- Applied to injuries to facilitate healing and prevent infection.
- Used around the nose to stop nose bleed.
- Used as an insect repellent when mixed with extra virgin olive oil.
- Help with insomnia when diffused or inhaled.
- Used to relieve acute chest discomfort and/or bronchitis by rubbing on the chest area.
- Used to help strengthen blood capillaries and increase circulation.

THIEVES™ OIL

(A blend of oils containing Clove, Lemon, Cinnamon Bark, Eucalyptus Radiata, and Rosemary)

Historical Uses:

- Blisters
- Canker sores
- Edema
- Toxic chemical absorption
- Sinus infection
- Tick bites
- Sore throat
- Liver disorders
- Colds
- Flu
- Mold
- Chicken pox
- Spider bite
- Malaria
- Whooping cough
- Thrombosis stroke

leader's notes

Session 6

HEALING AND REPENTANCE

GOALS:

- For you to understand that all diseases have causes.

- To understand there is a connection between unresolved emotions and physical disease, and that forgiveness is a necessary prelude to healing.

- To realize that repentance is necessary to prevent a return of disease once we are healed.

- To understand how essential oils can be used to access and resolve buried feelings that contribute to ill health.

- How anointing with oils while praying amplifies our intent and hastens healing.

KEY POINTS FROM SCRIPTURE

1. Diseases are not accidents. They all have causes.

2. There is a connection between forgiveness, repentance, and healing.

3. If we cannot forgive, then we cannot be forgiven. If we cannot be forgiven, then we cannot be healed.

4. Once healed, we must clear out the emotional and spiritual roots that brought illness upon us, otherwise our healing won't last and we may become worse than before.

5. And finally, we must repent to be healed, which means to change our life styles and habits, mentally and physically, in positive ways that will promote health and longevity.

A NOTE TO HOSTS:

As your group comes together to discuss the teachings from Dr. Stewart, some may be convicted by the Holy Spirit for the first time to take responsibility for the sin in their lives that has caused them illness. Some, on the other hand, may reject the teaching and take offense at what Scripture speaks so clearly on. As the host, by now you have come to know your group members. You can probably begin to anticipate some of their responses; and maybe not. You may be surprised at the workings of the Holy Spirit. In any case, you may need to take some time for sharing, being sensitive and loving to what some have just heard and what God is doing in their lives. There may be "healing tears" either in the teaching time or as you work through your discussion time. That is a good thing! The Good News is Jesus brings healing to those who confess, repent and forgive themselves, being made new through the power of the Holy Spirit. As a group, rejoice in the work God is doing in your group!

WRAP UP: The group shared some personal information and insights during this session. Take those insights and personal items to the Lord in prayer. Lead each one through a time of repentance and then assuring them in prayer the verse of James 5:16. Praying Scripture back to God, inserting personal names and requests is a powerful prayer time for the group to participate in. Rejoice in what God is doing, giving Him all the glory, honor and praise!

QUESTION 3. God has no limits on what He can do, however, we put limits on God. We will go more into this next week.

GIFTS DISCUSSED IN SESSION 6

HYSSOP

(hyssopus officinalis)

Historic Uses:

- Rubbed on the body or shoulders to reduce tension.
- Inhaled to loosen up a tight chest; it's highly expectorant.
- Hot compresses of hyssop oil have been found to be helpful for rheumatism and joint pain.
- Placed one drop on an injured area to help prevent scarring.
- Twentieth century physicians who used herbs in the United States used hyssop oil to soothe burned skin.
- Applied in cold compresses as soon as possible after bruising to help reduce the bruise.

- For the respiratory system, especially to help discharge toxins and mucus, diffused, applied to throat, chest, and feet.

GALBANUM (See Session 3)

FORGIVENESS™

(A blend of oils containing Sesame, Melissa, Geranium, Frankincense, Rosewood, Sandalwood, Angelica, Lavender, Lemon, Helichrysum, Jasmine, Roman Chamomile, Bergamot, Ylang Ylang, Palmarosa, Rose)

HARMONY™

(A blend of oils containing Geranium, Rosewood, Lavender, Sandalwood, Frankincense, Orange, Lemon, Angelica, Pine, Spruce, Hyssop, Spanish Sage, Jasmine, Roman Chamomile, Bergamot, Ylang Ylang, Rose)

leader's notes

Session 7
FAITH, LOVE, PRAYER, AND OILS

GOALS:

- To realize there are skills and attitudes to be developed in praying effectively for healing and that among them are persistence, boldness, love, and the cultivation of a personal, close relationship with God. These skills and attitudes are cultivated by spiritual work.

- To develop faith, pray from what you know and rest your faith on that. Then what you don't know will be revealed and your faith increased.

- Stimulate in you a desire to learn how anointing and other applications of essential oils can amplify your prayers and hasten healing in yourself and those for whom you pray.

- Inspire you to strive for a perpetual state of love and gratitude, because these are the natural states of consciousness for the children of God.

KEY POINTS FROM SCRIPTURE

1. God's instructions to Moses for a Holy Incense are accompanied with God's promise to meet with them where the aroma of the Incense is diffused.

2. Throughout the New Testament, God says in many ways, "Ask, and it will be given to you."

3. James says that when we do not receive it is because we do not ask. He goes on to say that we ask and do not receive because we ask wrongly.

4. Effective prayer includes not only faith and belief, but also boldness, thanksgiving, persistence, and the conviction that God hears us; that with our praying we have already received what we've prayed for.

5. The Bible teaches us to have confidence that through Christ we can do His works, and even greater works.

6. God is love and love is the open channel through which God's healing power flows freely.

ADDITIONAL SCRIPTURES IN DVD TEACHING

Luke 18:1-5; Luke 11:5-8

"Facilitate the group discussion in a loving manner that is encouraging; especially to those who still have doubts. This session serves well to help those who have doubts or are struggling in their faith. There is no disgrace in doubts. Remember to add these to your closing prayer time."

WRAP UP: Lead the group through a time of asking God to increase the faith of each member of your group. Ask God to help them to let go and allow Him to be in control of their life, physically, emotionally and spiritually. Thank Him for all the gifts He has given to provide health and healing. Remember to pray on what you know to be true of God. Thank Him in advance for answering all your prayers. Pray with expectation, believing you have already received what you have asked God for!

GIFTS DISCUSSED IN SESSION 7

ROSE OF SHARON

also know as CISTUS (*Cistus ladanifer*)

Historical Uses:

- Applied to area where arthritis pain occurs.
- Applied 4 or 5 drops along the spine to help with infection.
- Diluted with olive oil and applied to the face for wrinkles.
- Put a few drops on chest with vegetable oil for bronchitis.
- Applied to wrist, inside elbows, temples, soles of the feet, and inhale.
- Cistus is high in phenols and may strengthen and support the immune system.

SPIKENARD

(*Nardostachys jatamansi*)

Historical Uses:

· Used to soften skin and rough or wrinkled skin when mixed with extra virgin olive oil.
· Diluted 50/50 with extra virgin olive oil and apply on location for help with hemorrhoids.
· In India, one drop is taken near the end of a meal to calm the stomach.
· Inhale to reduce feelings of fear or anxiety.

VALOR®

(See Session 1)

leader's notes

Session 8

THE GREAT COMMISSION AND BEYOND

GOALS:

- To inspire you to diligently seek the Great Commission God has in mind for you and that you plunge into it with confidence, faith, courage, and energy, seeking always to express the best and most suitable gifts.

- To never stop praying and working on yourself, spiritually, so that your gifts will constantly improve and grow in God's service to humankind.

- To know that you do have the gift of healing if you choose it and desire to develop it through diligence and devotional practice.

KEY POINTS FROM SCRIPTURE

1. The last two verses of Matthew (28:19-20) are often called "The Great Commission."

2. There are also Great Commissions expressed in Mark 6 and 16, as well as in Luke 10, I Peter 2, and James 5.

3. We are told that whatever we ask in prayer, and believe, it will be ours.

4. We are to pray and speak with all boldness and the Lord will heal and perform signs and wonders through us in the holy name of Jesus.

5. You are a member of a chosen race destined to serve God in mighty ways.

Encourage and celebrate those who feel called and led to share this study with others. Help them work through the details and share with them all you have learned as a host that would contribute to their success. Rejoice that God is spreading the word of one of His most amazing forgotten gifts: healing. Imagine the lives that will be touched, renewed and transformed through God's Holy Spirit!

WRAP UP: Allow some time at the end, if this has not happened already, to share the miracles and celebrate what God has done in the lives of your group members. End this study praising God and thanking Him for each individual and the miracles He has already done and will continue to do in the days, weeks and months ahead. Ask God for opportunities to share what you've learned with others.

GIFTS DISCUSSED IN SESSION 8

Exodus II™

(See Session 3)

Joy^{TM}

(See session 1)

Finalize the details for next week's celebration if your group has chosen to do so. Celebrate what God has done!

A FINAL NOTE FOR HOSTS:

Thank you for taking the time to lead a group through this study! We value your input and would love it if you would share testimonies from your group. Please remember to respect the confidentiality of your group members. We are looking for sharing as to what happened within the group, like where you saw God working and the life-changing transformation that has come about as a result of this study. Any personal testimonies should only be placed by the person themselves at their own discretion. There is a place for this on www.godsforgottengift.com under the "Stories of Healing" tab. Please know that we, too, are rejoicing with you before the Lord for revealing His miraculous gifts, especially God's forgotten gift of healing. God bless you!

RESOURCES

The following books and DVDs are valuable adjuncts to *Healing: God's Forgotten Gift*.

Healing Oils of the Bible (both book and DVD) are the foundation resources for the whole program, *Healing: God's Forgotten Gift*. For serious applications of essential oils for healing purposes, you will need at least one of the first two resources listed and marked with asterisks (*), the **Essential Oil Desk Reference* or the **Reference Guide to Essential Oils*. These two contain encyclopedic information on specific applications of essential oils for specific conditions or diseases.

The Chemistry book in the list is unique in that is not only easy to understand without any background in chemistry, it is written with a Biblical basis and demonstrates how anointing for healing with essential oils is both scriptural and scientific. This book provides a scientific basis for *"Healing: God's Forgotten Gift."*

All of the resources listed here can be purchased on the internet at www.RaindropTraining.com, as well as many other places, except for the books by MacNutt. The books by Francis MacNutt, as well as *Healing Oils of the Bible*, are available in most Christian bookstores.

BOOKS

Essential Oil Desk Reference, edited by Brian Manwaring
Reference Guide to Essential Oils by Connie and Alan Higley
A More Excellent Way by Henry Wright
Chemistry of Essential Oils Made Simple (God's Love Manifest in Molecules) by David Stewart
Feelings Buried Alive Never Die by Karol Truman
Gentle Babies by Debra Rayburn
Heal Your Body by Louise Hay
Healing by Francis MacNutt
Healing Oils of the Bible by David Stewart
Healing Oils — Healing Hands by Linda Smith
Molecules of Emotion by Candace Pert
The Power to Heal by Francis MacNutt
The Prayer that Heals by Francis MacNutt
Releasing Emotional Patterns with Essential Oils by Carolyn Mein
Scriptural Essence: Temple Secrets Revealed by Janet McBride

BOOKLETS

Quantum Physics, Essential Oils, and the Mind-Body Connection by David Stewart

DVDS

Chemistry of Essential Oils Made Simple by David Stewart
Emotional Releasing with Oils by David Stewart
Healing Oils of the Bible by David Stewart

Class Resources

HEALTH ASSESSMENT

Spiritual well-being					
I have a strong spiritual connection to God through regular prayer time.	1	2	3	4	5
I am growing in my ability to share and show love to those around me.	1	2	3	4	5
I seek out opportunities to forgive.	1	2	3	4	5
I am accepting things that I cannot change and place my trust in God's hands.	1	2	3	4	5
Emotional well-being					
I take time to laugh.	1	2	3	4	5
I cultivate a spiritual relationship with God.	1	2	3	4	5
I am willing to share the emotional challenges I face.	1	2	3	4	5
I am experiencing more of God's presence in my life.	1	2	3	4	5
Physical well-being					
I am consciously aware of what I eat each day.	1	2	3	4	5
I know why I take medication and possible side affects.	1	2	3	4	5
I am physically doing something healthy for my body at least three times a week.	1	2	3	4	5
I treat my body like a Holy Temple.	1	2	3	4	5

My Family well-being					
My family is healthy model to follow.	I	2	3	4	5
My family encourages open communication.	I	2	3	4	5
My family resolves emotional conflicts quickly and easily.	I	2	3	4	5
My family attends a worship center or church at least once a month	I	2	3	4	5.
My Community well being					
I serve as a regular volunteer in the community or worship center at least once a month.	I	2	3	4	5
I contribute financially where I practice my faith.	I	2	3	4	5
I consider myself a team player in my small group.	I	2	3	4	5
I am a willing mentor.	I	2	3	4	5

Knowledgeable	Sharing	Learning	Not a Clue
16-20	12-16	6-12	1-6

Pre-small group score _____   Post small group score _____

Group Agreement

We are shaped in a life giving community through these values:

Christ Centered
Other Focused
Mission Ready
Messengers of Truth
Unity as One
Nurturing
Impactful through Prayer, Words & Actions
Teachable and Willing to Teach Others
Yes Attitude for God's Plan

As a part of this community, I pledge together to uphold these values and agree to the following personal commitments:

☐ Availability – at group gatherings and in meeting others' needs
☐ Confidentiality – issues discussed held confidential within group
☐ Respect – words that build up others and not tear them down
☐ Authentic – openness to be myself and allow others to do the same
☐ Truthful – permission to allow others to tell me the truth

Additional pledge items:

_____

_____

_____

_____

Signed: Date: _____

Small Group Calendar

Healthy groups share responsibilities and group ownership. It may take some time for this to fully develop. From the very beginning of your group, encourage everyone to look over this calendar and choose a way to participate. Explain how if the responsibilities are shared, then it's easier for everyone. For example, if someone has the group at their home, then someone else brings the snack, while another person facilitates or leads the discussion (taking the video home with them to prepare), and another person leads the group in prayer. This way no one feels an undue burden. By taking turns, leadership is developed. Your small group is a safe environment in which to learn and grow. Planning ahead will increase attendance and help everyone to enjoy a successful small group experience.

Date	Lesson	Location	Facilitator	Snack	Prayer
	Session 1				
	Session 2				
	Session 3				
	Session 4				
	Session 5				
	Session 6				
	Session 7				
	Session 8				
	Celebration!				

Small Group Prayer and Praise Report

Date	Person	Prayer Request	Praise Report

Small Group Roster

Name	Phone	E-Mail
1		
2		
3		
4		
5		
6		
7		
8		
9		
10		
11		
12		

ABOUT THE AUTHORS

David Stewart, Ph.D., D.N.M. holds degrees in Math, Physics, Earth Sciences, Natural Medicine, and Aromatic Science. A former professor at the University of North Carolina, Chapel Hill, and Southeast Missouri State University. He is the author of 16 books and more than 300 articles. His latest book and five-hour DVD set of the same name are entitled *The Chemistry of Essential Oils Made Simple.* Dr. Stewart is President of the Center for Aromatherapy Research and Education (CARE), offering more than 100 seminars each year on the science and practical application of essential oils throughout the United States, Canada, and other selected countries. For more information on Dr. Stewart and his classes visit www.raindroptraining.com

 **Don Clair Ph.D.c,** and his wife Roberta Jane have six adult children and currently reside in Waterloo, IL. Over the past two decades Don has designed and delivered cognitive behavior coaching programs for individuals and corporations. He is a member of the International Council for Human Rights of Children. He is a member of the International Council for Human Rights of Children and an active member of Faith Lutheran Church. He is a powerful and insightful keynote speaker and has presented material in several cultures nationally and internationally. He has written three books titled *Mastering Influence, Secrets From Behind the Wall,* and a new novel *The Longest Monday.*

For more information on Don please visit: www.claircaringcenter.com.

Sandy Sutter has written many Bible studies, articles and devotions over the past 25 years. She has taught numerous Bible classes for children, teens and adults. An active small group leader in Faith Lutheran Church, Oakville, MO, Sandy has also served on the church staff and other leadership positions. A wife of 33 years and a mother of three grown children, Sandy and her husband, Norm, along with their son, Wade, own and operate Fresh Pasture Farms, a pastured poultry and egg farm in southern Illinois.

To contact Sandy or to learn more about their farm visit: www.freshpasturefarms.com.

Cover Art designed by Matt Clair at www.mattclair.com.

Where to Obtain Biblical Grade Oils for Healing

You will need good and pure essential oils to engage in the healing mission described in this book and DVD. Otherwise you can't expect the results you should receive. Most essential oils available in retail stores and other places are perfume or food grade oils and do not have the chemistry and other properties necessary for therapeutic applications. Therefore to obtain the healing results intended by this book and DVD, you need to be sure you are obtaining Biblical grade therapeutic essential oils raised without chemical fertilizers and without insecticides or pesticides. They also must have been extracted by distillation at minimum temperatures and pressures and without any chemical solvents, as was done in Biblical times. One company that specializes in such quality is Young Living Essential Oils, Inc., whose website is www.youngliving.com and whose phone number is (800) 371-3515.

You will need a sponsor to order directly from this company. If you have a friend or relative, or perhaps the leader of your Bible study group, who is a distributor with Young Living, they can be your sponsor. Otherwise, you can request one of the three authors of this book to be your sponsor. You can enroll via the website or phone number above or you can contact the person directly whom you have chosen to be your sponsor.

As a Young Living distributor you can order directly from the company at wholesale prices and can be assured that you are receiving the highest quality of pure, Biblical grade, essential oils available. You may also sponsor others. You may also visit www.godsforgottengift.com for information on enrolling with Young Living. All of the trademarked oil blends mentioned in this program are formulated and available only from Young Living Essential Oils.

ANSWERS FOR THE FILL-IN BLANKS

The answers for the blanks, as heard from the DVD, are as follows:

Session 1

God's Gift from the Beginning (p. 5)
freedom
will
freedom
earnest desire
fervent prayer
healers
God

Session 2

Oils and Healing (p. 11)
anoint with oils
study
learn
use them
known
ask for healing
move on
touch
hearts

Session 3

Oils for Spiritual Purposes (p. 18)
pray for guidance
whisper to you

essential oils
made

Session 4

Cedarwood and Solomon (p. 25)
faith
healing
thinking
minds

Session 5

Oils, Temple Maintenance & Repair (pp. 31-32)
We are
We are
We are
We are
We are
We are
We are
It is us and nobody else

Session 6

Healing and Repentance (p. 38)
forgive
forgiven
recognize
responsibility
reverse
unforgiveness
action

life change
repentance

Session 7

Faith, Love Prayer and Oils (p. 46)
 iaomai (Greek. pronounced eh-o-meh) *
sozo (Greek. pronounced zo-tso)*
therapeuo(Greek. pronounced the-rah-pay-vo)*
well
gratitude
love
* See pp. 91-92 in the book, Healing Oils of the Bible.

Session 8

The Great Commission and Beyond (p. 54)
Great Commissions
Anoint with oils
Lay on hands
Pray
Cast out demons
stick to the mission
pray
chosen
healing